# KAREL HUSA

# CONCERTO

## for Violoncello and Orchestra

*Winner of the 1993 University of Louisville Grawemeyer Award for Music Composition*

AMP 8129
First printing: June 1998

ISBN 0-7935-8274-1

Associated Music Publishers, Inc.

DISTRIBUTED BY
HAL•LEONARD®
CORPORATION
7777 W. BLUEMOUND RD. P.O. BOX 13819 MILWAUKEE, WI 53213

# PROGRAM NOTE

As a young student I played violin, but when I entered the Prague Conservatory in 1940, I was immediately exposed to the solo cello as my teacher, the important Czech composer Jaroslav Ridky, was composing his second Concerto. There is a great tradition in Prague for both composition and solo performance on the cello. Not only Dvořák, but composers such as Voříšek, Stamitz, Mysliveček, Vranický, and Kraft—all have written concertos for this instrument.

After the war, I left Prague to pursue studies in Paris and had the chance to hear the great cellists of the French School. Yet, until now, I have only written for this five-octave-range instrument in chamber and orchestral music. It was a great pleasure, then, to be invited to write a concerto for Lynn Harrell, whose playing I have admired for a long time.

Because of the rich literature for this instrument, many of the unusual sonorities, the advanced techniques, and use of the extreme high register have already been explored in other works (especially when we include harmonics, which extend the range even higher). Hopefully, I have found some new paths, but mostly I have been concerned with writing music that would belong to our time, music of today. Naturally, as the title suggests, a concerto is a work in which the virtuosic and technical aspects of the solo part, as well as the dialogue between the soloist and the orchestra, are of great importance. Also, I hope, it will reflect the enjoyment of music making and listening, the excitement of living in this world of much progress, yet with such basic problems as freedom and respect for man and nature unfulfilled.

The concerto is composed in five parts. In the first, "Introduction," the solo cello begins in the lowest register, in unison with the cello section of the orchestra. Progressively, it detaches itself to become an independent voice and performs soloistically in the following "Recitative." "Anecdote" is a scherzo movement in which the soloist plays pizzicato throughout. "Remembrance" is a slow, meditative movement. The last part is a "Hymn," climaxing at the conclusion, in which the solo cello soars up to its highest register, perhaps reminiscent of a flight of birds—albatross comes to my mind—but it would be presumptuous to think one could succeed in appropriately expressing such a magnificent exploit.

The *Concerto for Violoncello and Orchestra* was composed in 1987–88 in Ithaca, New York.

—KAREL HUSA

# Instrumentation

Solo Cello

3 Flutes (3rd doubling Piccolo)
3 Oboes (3rd doubling English Horn)
2 Clarinets in B♭
Bass Clarinet
2 Bassoons
Contrabassoon

4 Horns in F
3 Trumpets in C
3 Trombones
Tuba

Timpani (5 drums)
Percussion (three players):
    Vibraphone, Marimba, Xylophone, Glockenspiel, Chimes, Suspended Cymbals
    (small & large), Crash Cymbals, Large Gong, Bass Drum, Snare Drum, Tom-
    toms, Temple Blocks, Wood Blocks

Harp (doubled)

Strings

*Duration: ca. 27 minutes*

*Commissioned by the School of Music of the University of Southern California.*

*This commission is dedicated to Frank Kerze Jr.*
*by his sisters, Therese Kerze Cheyovich and Florence Kerze.*

*Premiere performance: March 2, 1989, University of Southern California,*
*the University of Southern California Symphony*
*Lynn Harrell, cello, Daniel Lewis, conductor*

**A full score is available for purchase separately (order no. 50482581).**

**Performance material is available on rental from the publisher.**

# Performance Notes

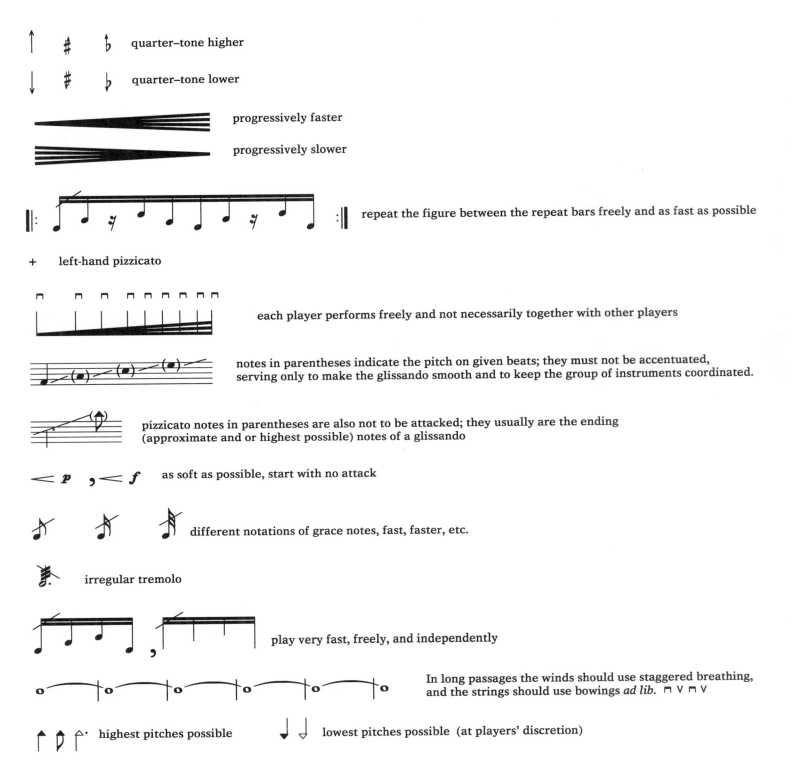

↑ ♯ ♭  quarter–tone higher

↓ ♯ ♭  quarter–tone lower

progressively faster

progressively slower

repeat the figure between the repeat bars freely and as fast as possible

+    left-hand pizzicato

each player performs freely and not necessarily together with other players

notes in parentheses indicate the pitch on given beats; they must not be accentuated,
serving only to make the glissando smooth and to keep the group of instruments coordinated.

pizzicato notes in parentheses are also not to be attacked; they usually are the ending
(approximate and or highest possible) notes of a glissando

as soft as possible, start with no attack

different notations of grace notes, fast, faster, etc.

irregular tremolo

play very fast, freely, and independently

In long passages the winds should use staggered breathing,
and the strings should use bowings *ad lib.*

highest pitches possible          lowest pitches possible  (at players' discretion)

Metronome markings are approximate.

# CONCERTO
## FOR VIOLONCELLO AND ORCHESTRA
### I. Introduction

Karel Husa
(1988)

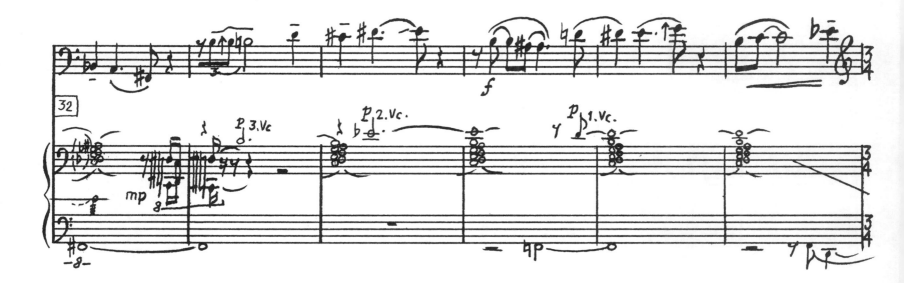

1) *The "A" will start p (progr. cresc. to the Recitatif )*

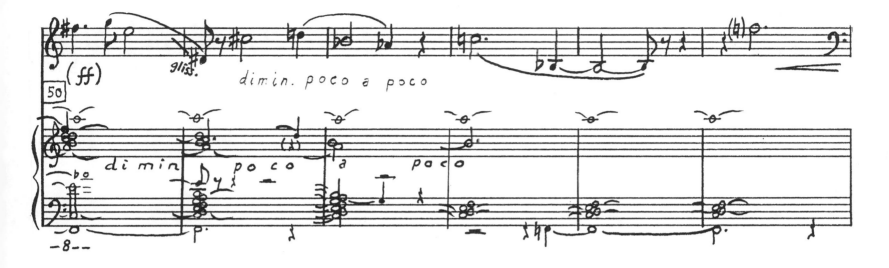

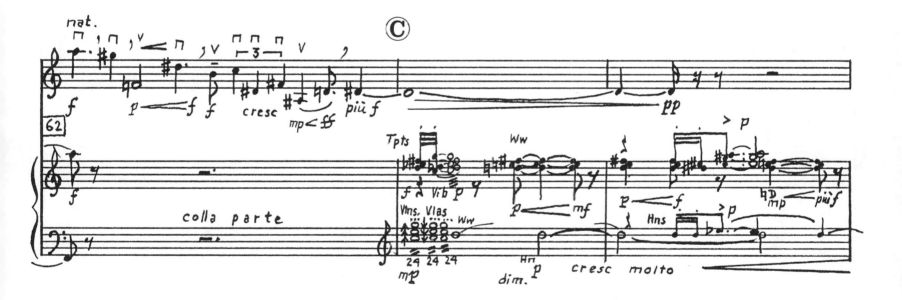

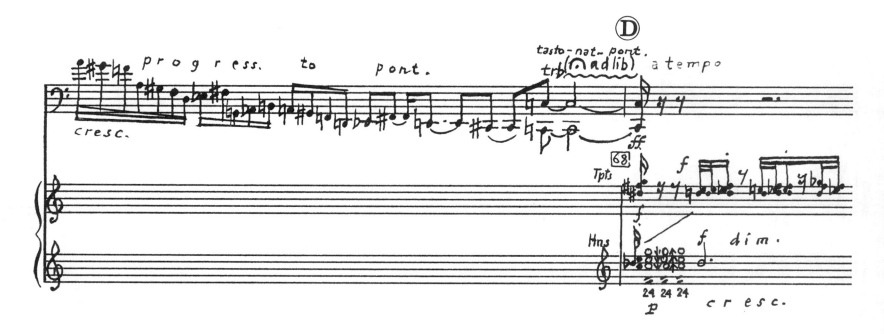

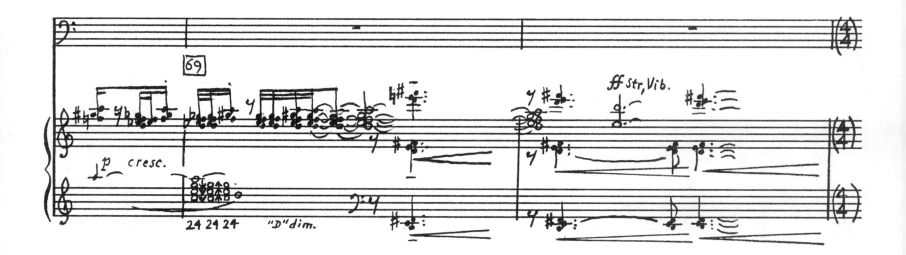

attacca

## II. Recitative

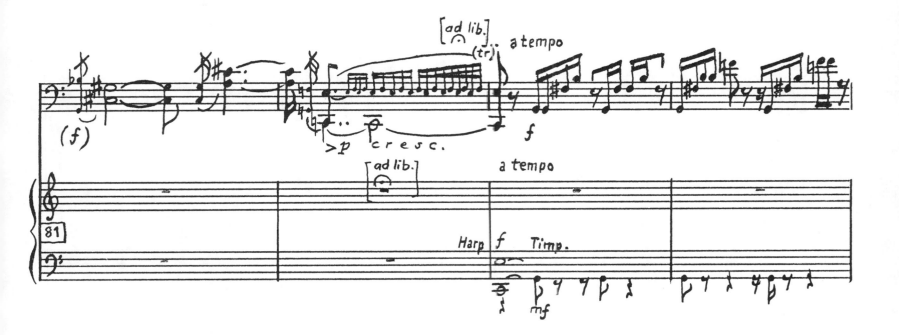

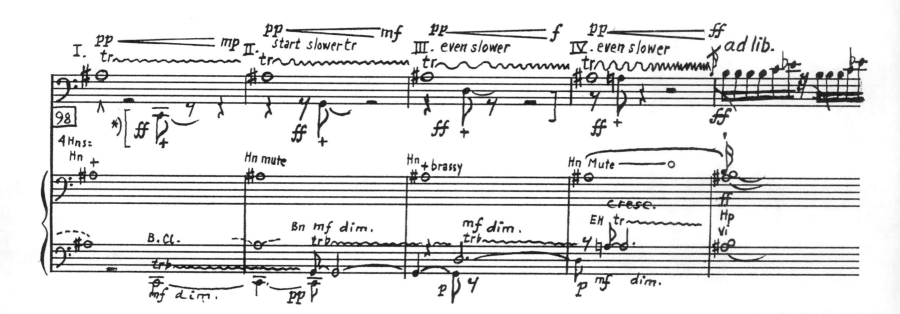

to nat.

progress. to point-

104

to tasto

108

*) may be played by 1.solo (orchestra)

112

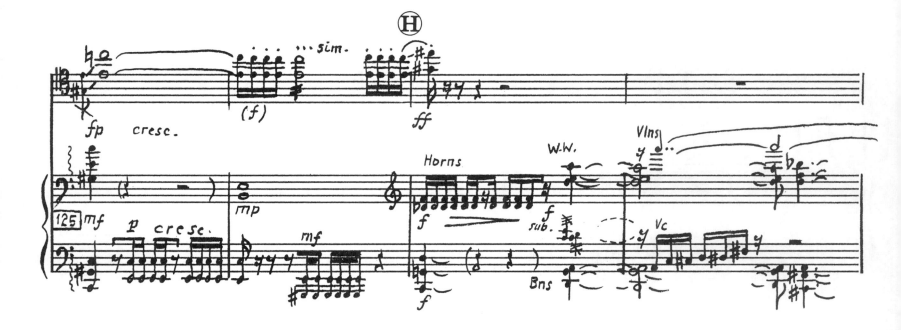

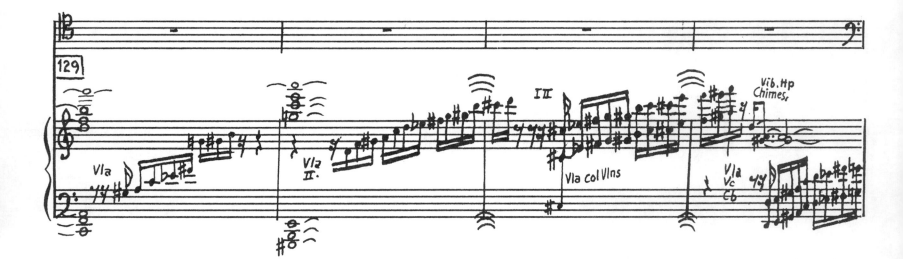

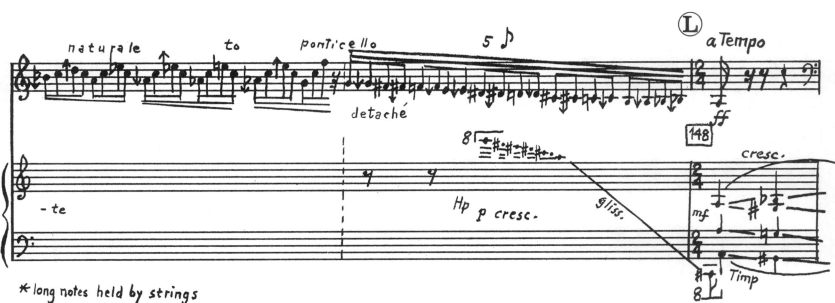

* long notes held by strings

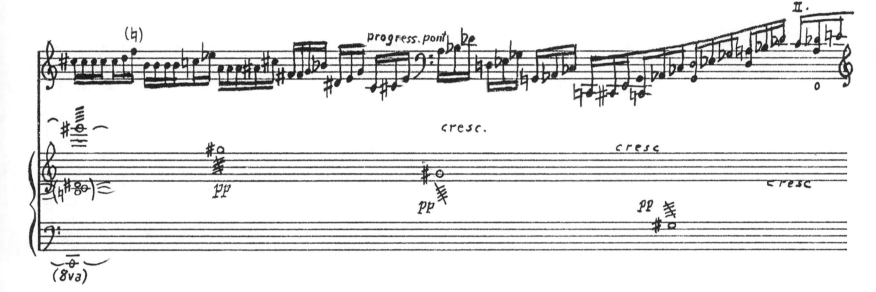

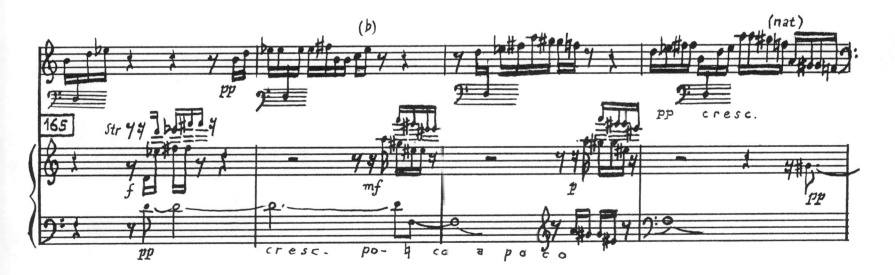

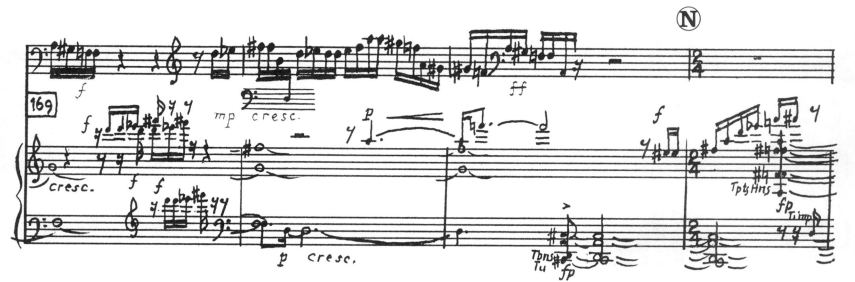

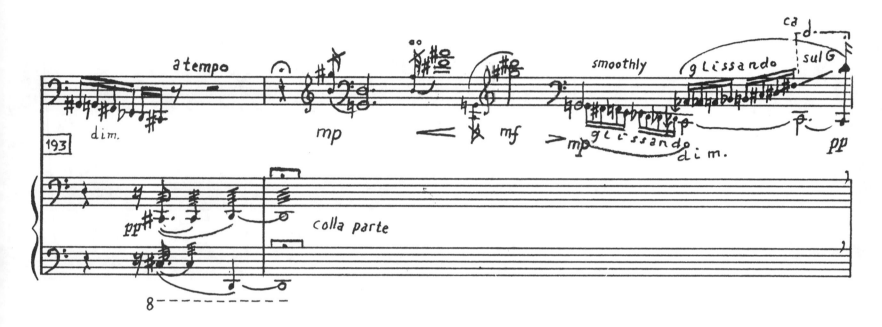

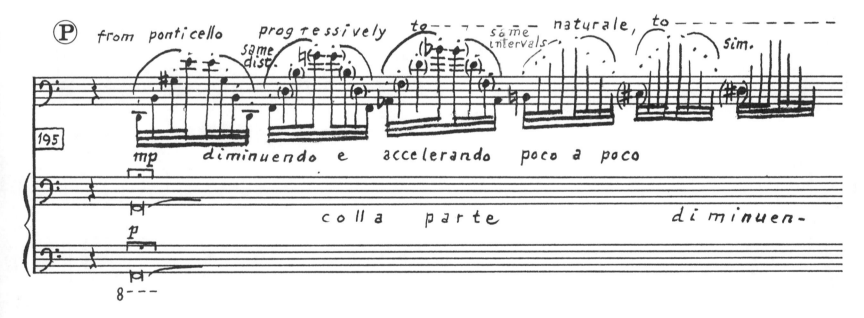

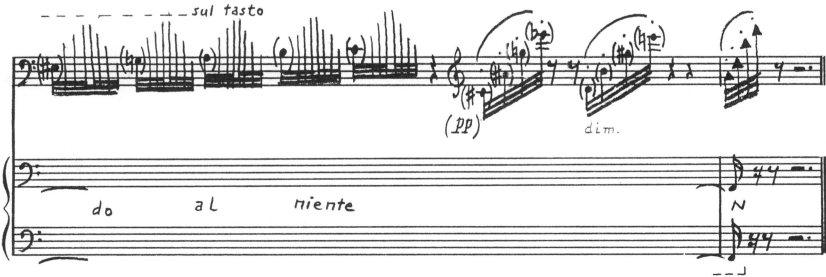

# III. Anecdote

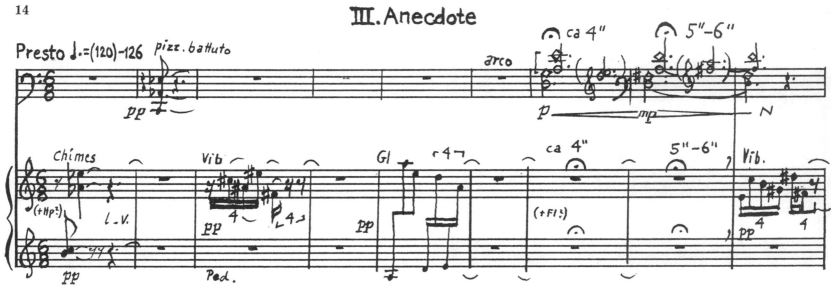

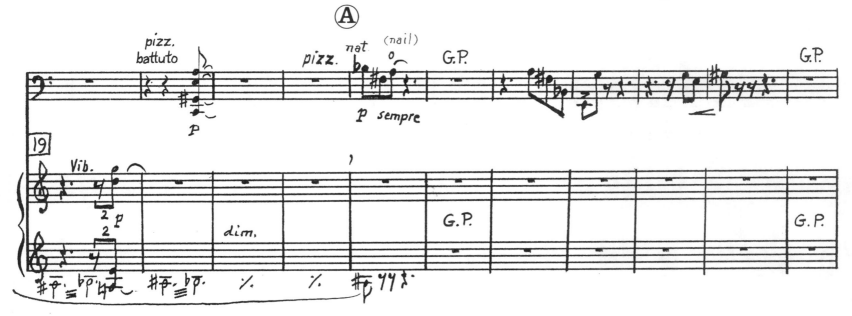

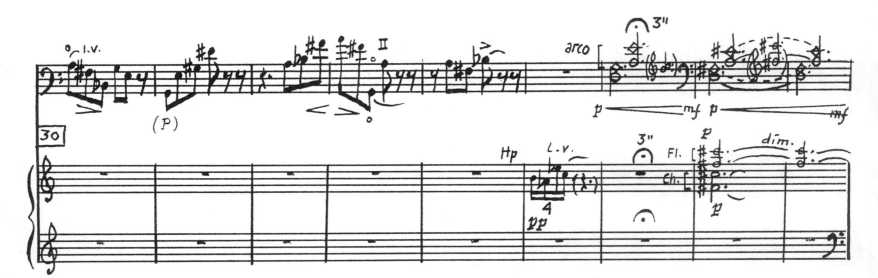

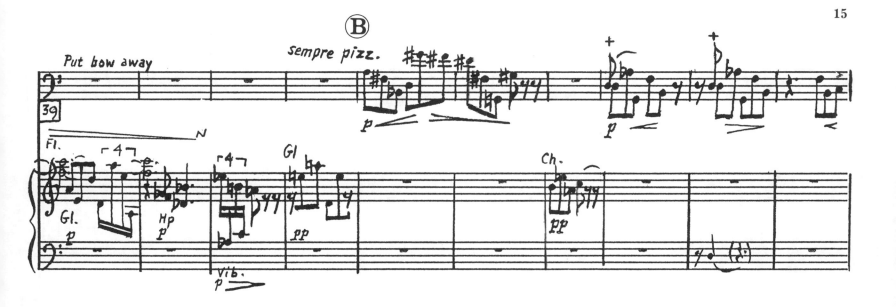

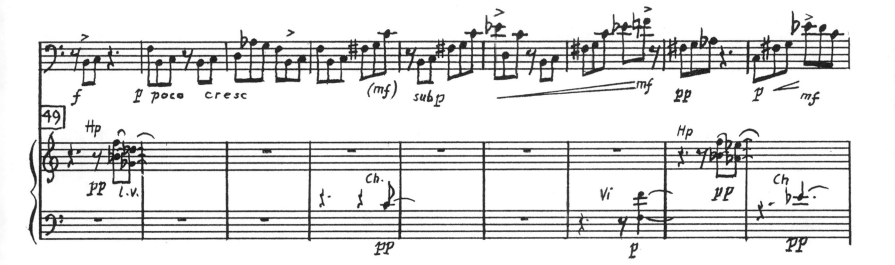

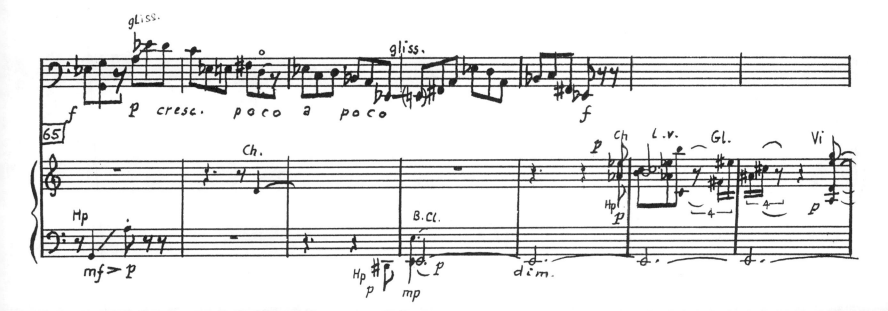

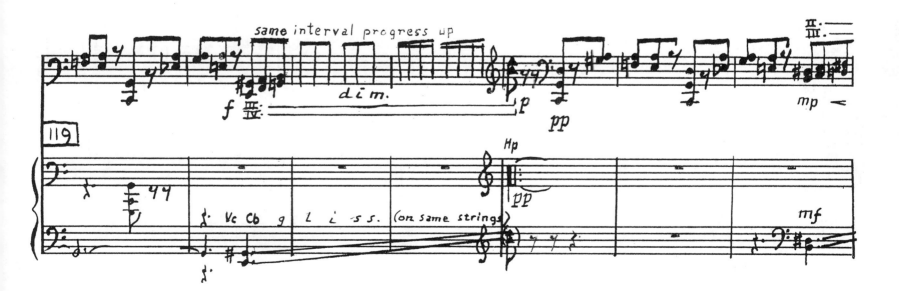

18

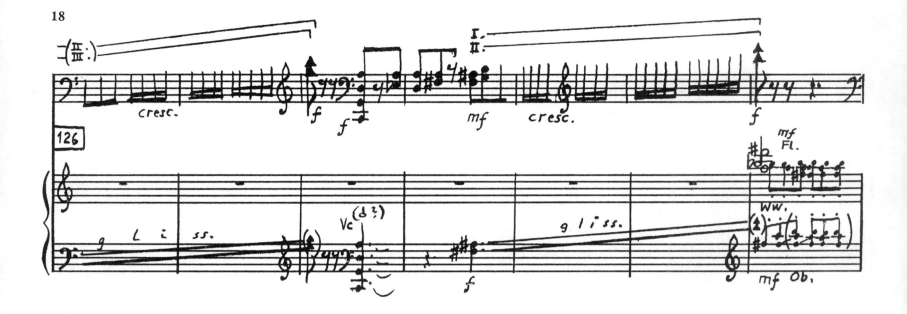

1) approx. pitches ( ▲ –highest on given string[s])

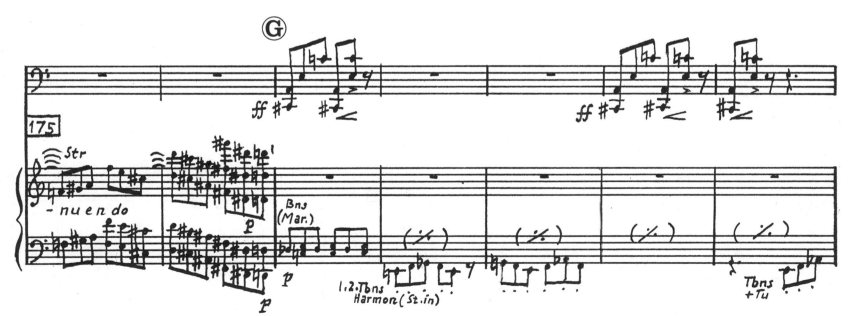

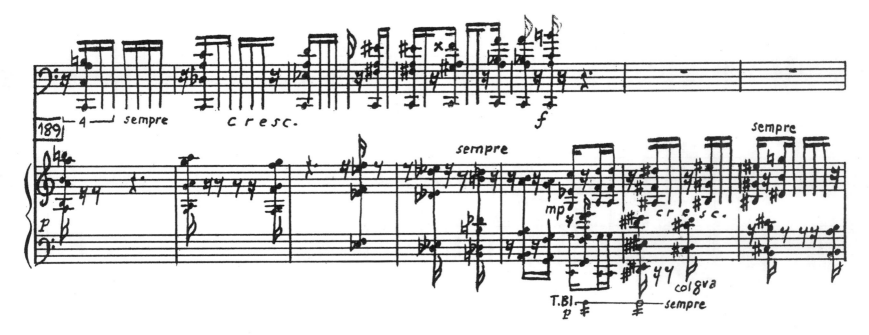

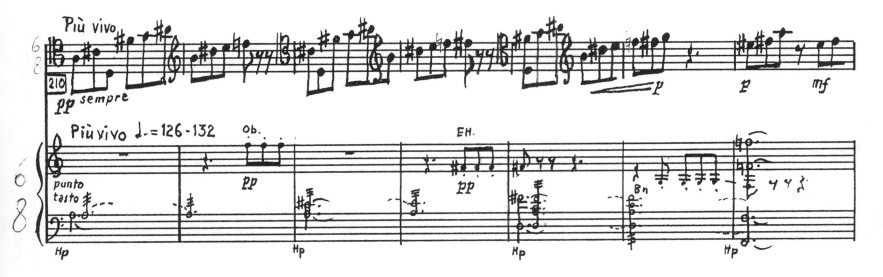

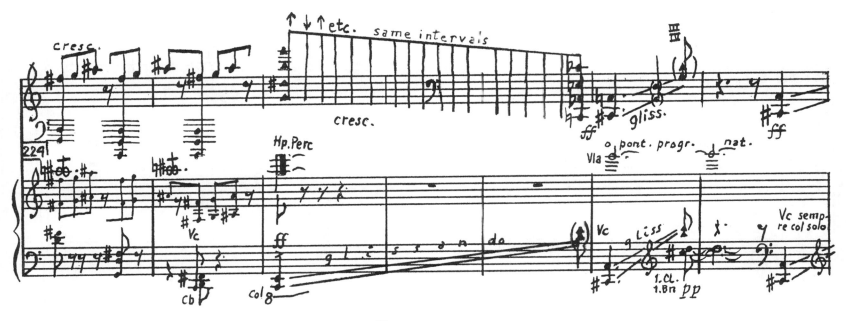

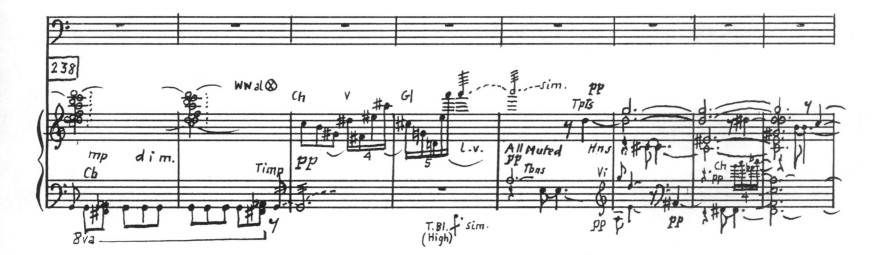

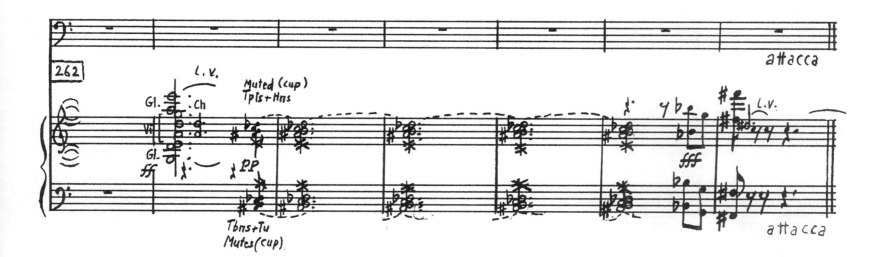

# IV. Remembrance

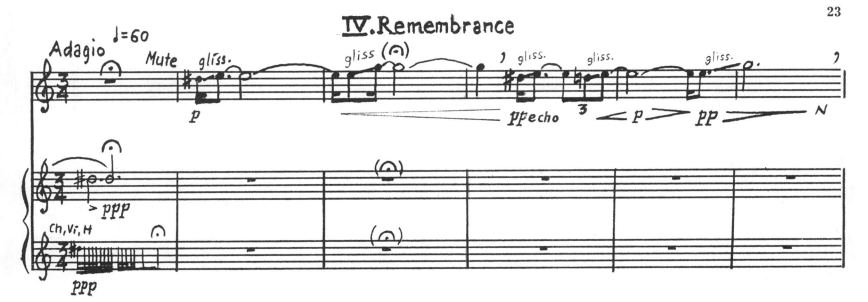

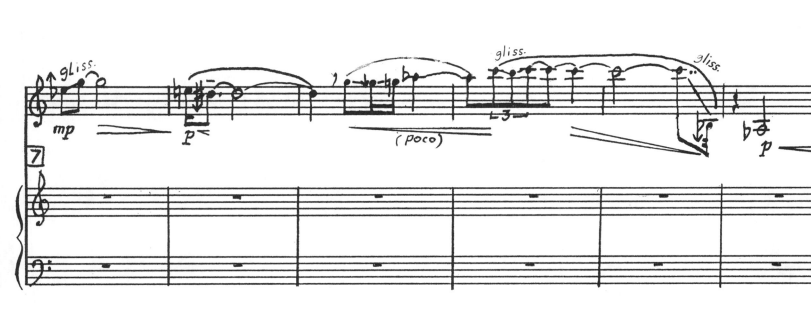

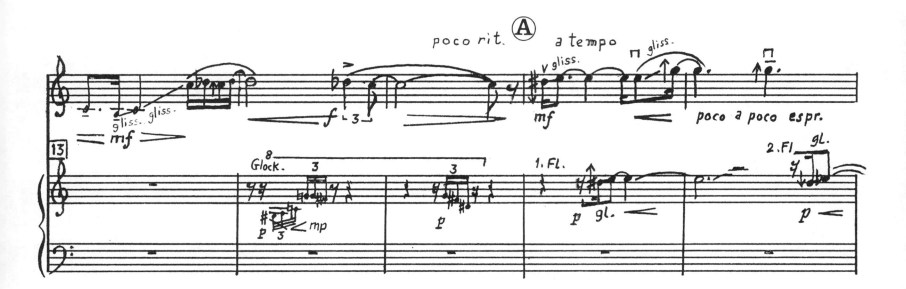

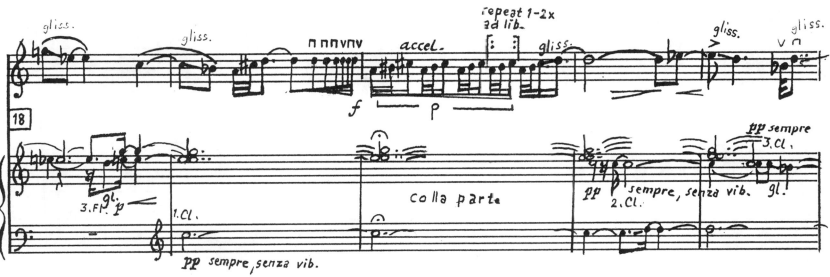

*) see footnote p.7

# V. Hymn

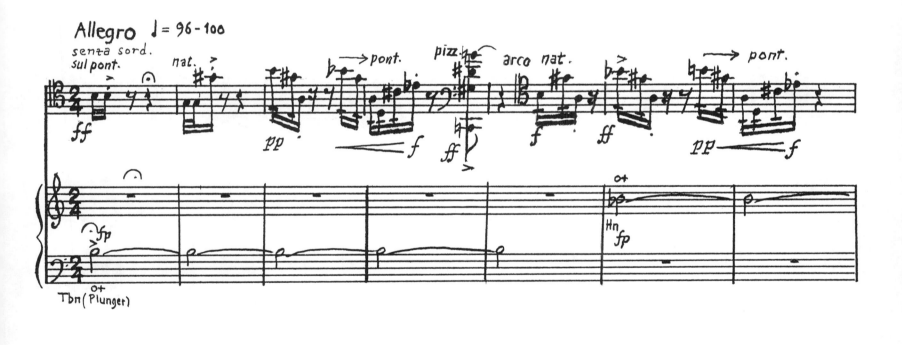

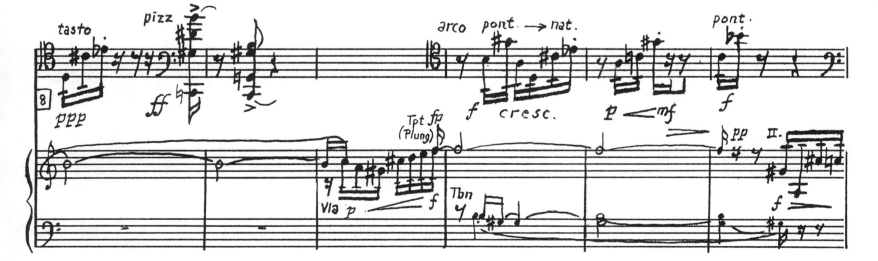

28

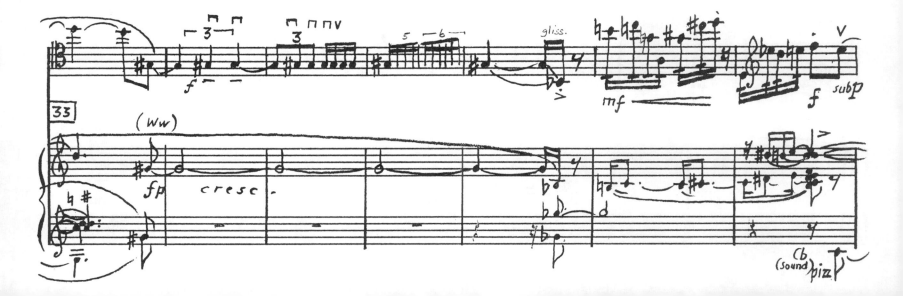

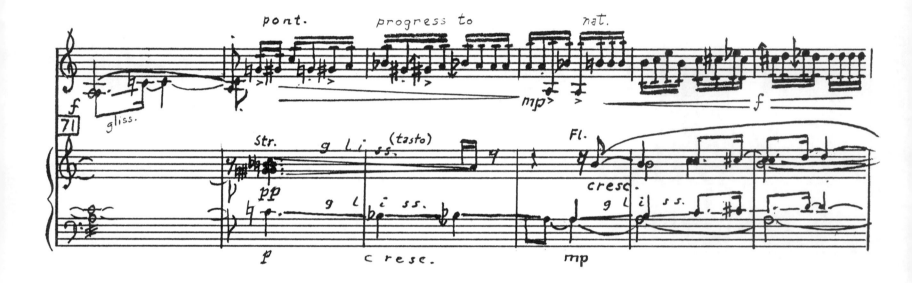

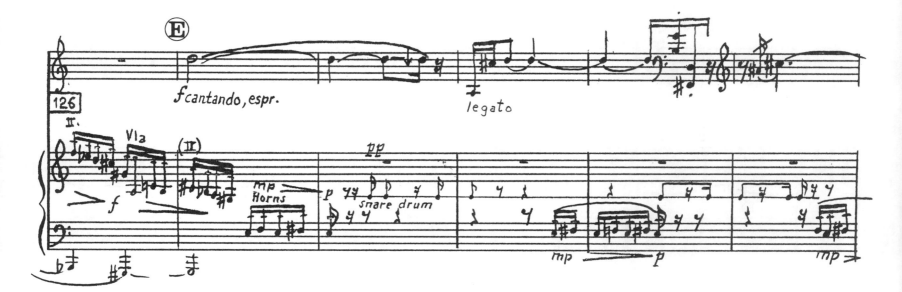

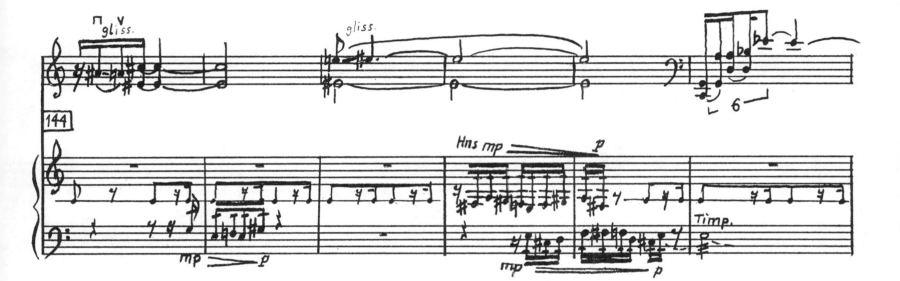

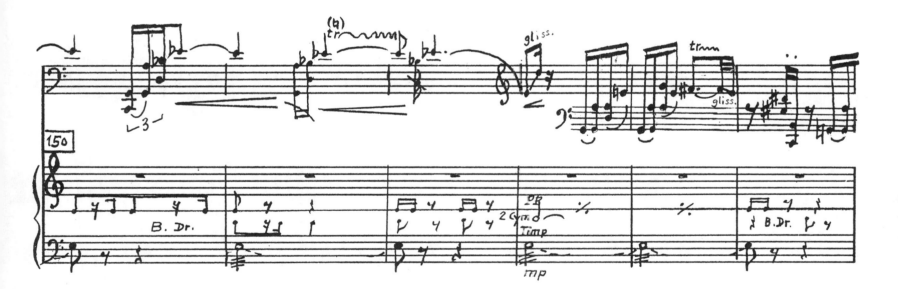

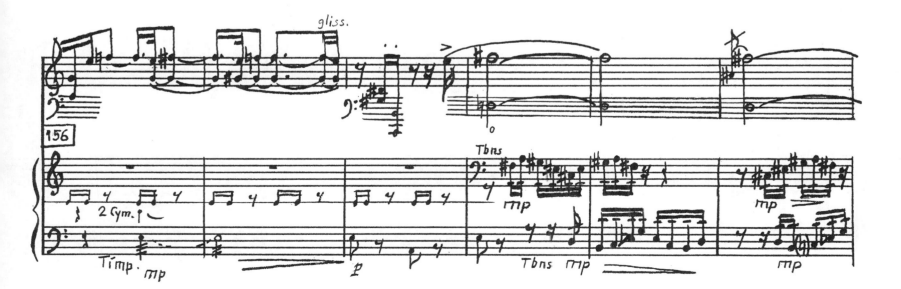

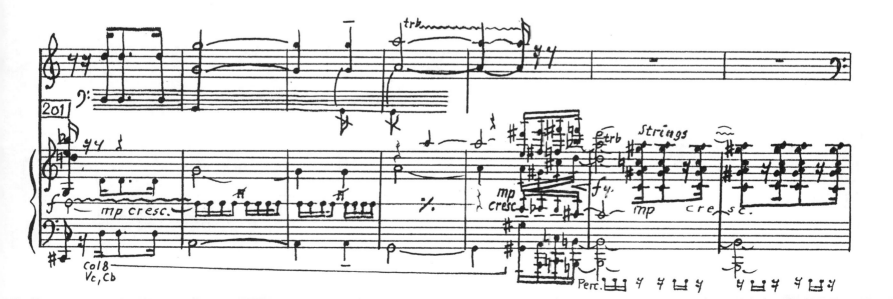

1) freely, the 1st and last note must be in place

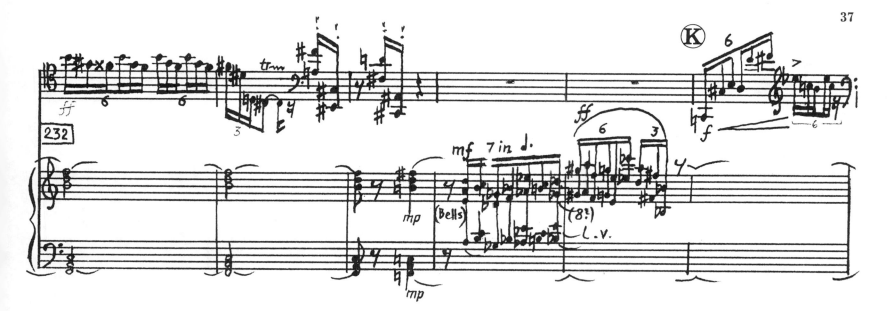

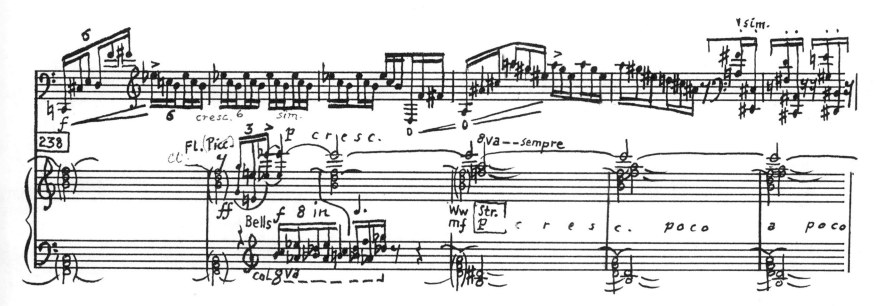

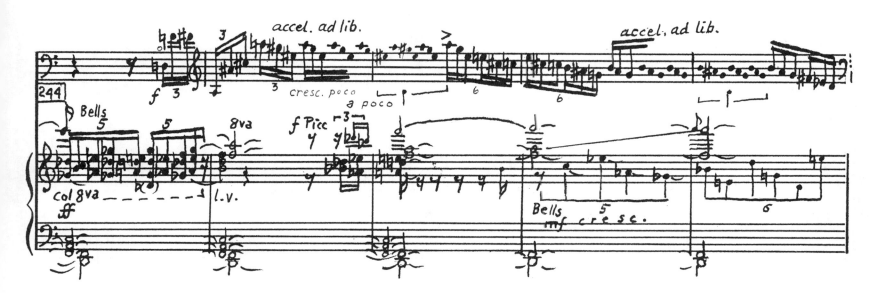

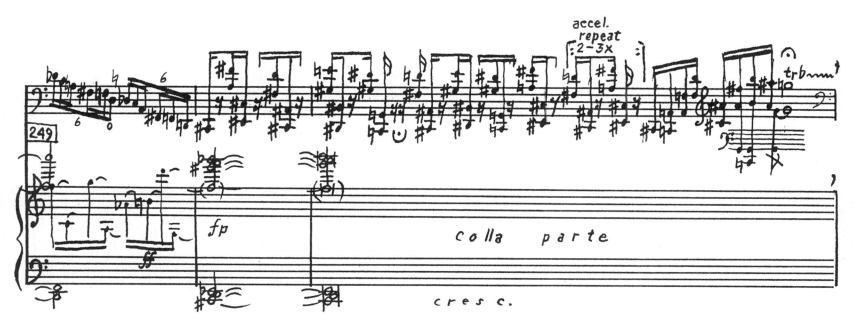

Maestoso ♩=66+

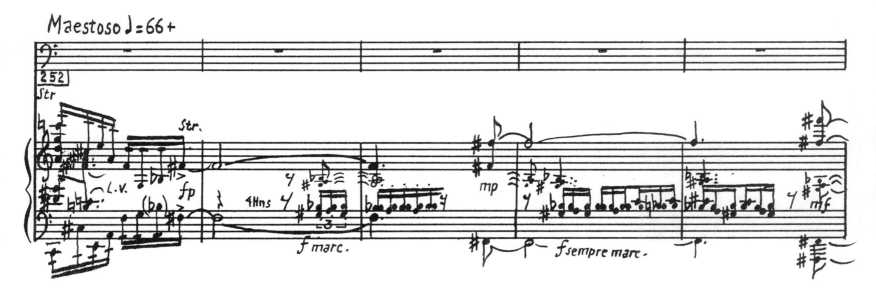

Ⓛ

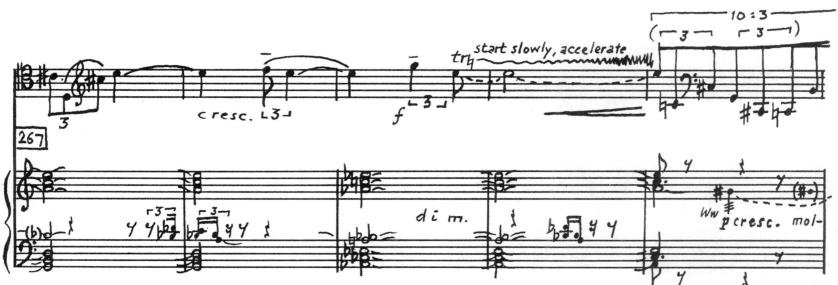

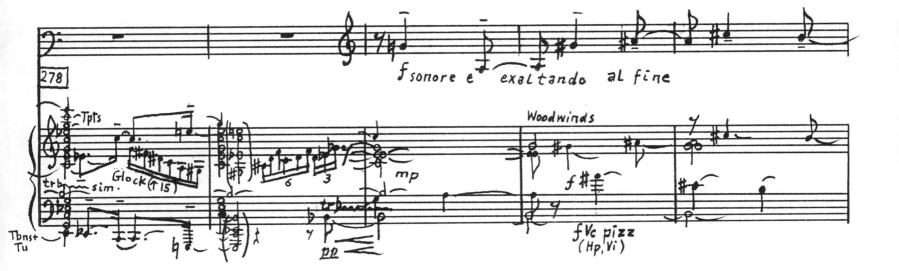

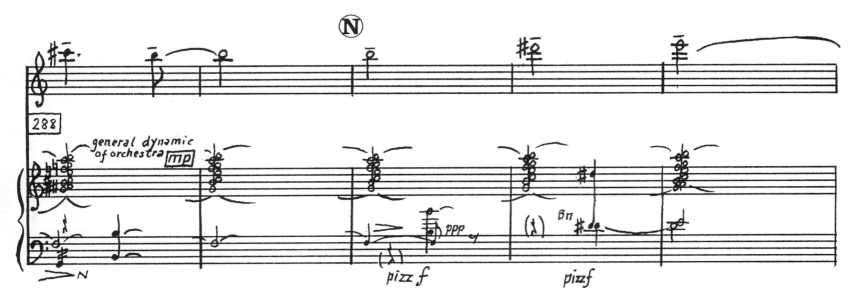

40

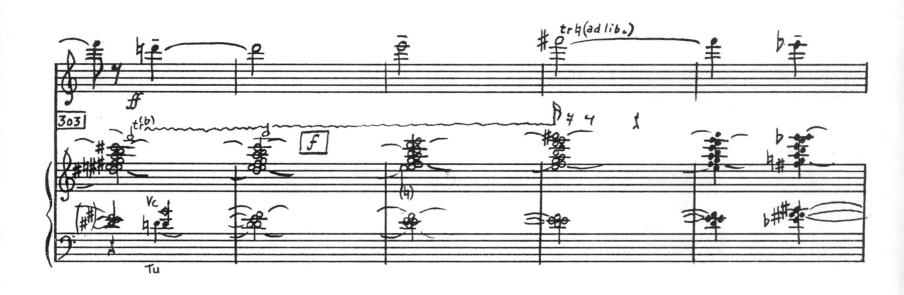

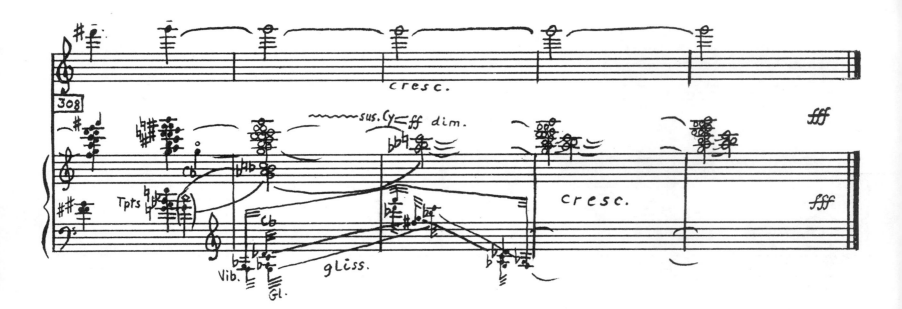